Tom Brady

A Biography of an NFL Superstar

Table of Contents

Introduction

Brady sat with his teammates at halftime with their heads down. It was the Super Bowl, and they were being torn apart by the Matt Ryan-led Atlanta Falcons. Their offense had stalled, and their defense shredded, and the result was a 21-3 deficit at halftime. Some New England fans had already started leaving. Brady had wanted to win for his mom, who had been out with cancer for the better part of the last year. She was in the stands for her first game after a year, and he was being dominated right in front of her. He would win. He knew he would.

Bill Belichick stood in the middle of the team and told them all they had to do was play better than they did in the first half.

Yes, they had to do better. Brady reinforced the coach's words to his teammates. All they had to do was play better. In the third quarter of the second half, they had fallen into a bigger deficit at 28-3, and everyone concluded it was over. Brady was widely considered to be the best quarterback in the league, but no one saw how he could come out of this one victorious. The New England fans were beginning to leave, and some teammates had their heads down, but Brady believed. And the miracle started midway into the third quarter.

Brady led the offense on a 13-play, 75-yard drive, finding running back James White for their first touchdown to end the third quarter.

Atlanta punted at the start of the fourth quarter, and Brady mounted another long drive that bled, ending in a Gostkowski field goal to cut the score back to 28-12. A possible comeback still seemed impossible as there were only 9 minutes and 44 seconds left on the clock. However, the momentum began to change, and the few Patriots fans still left in the stadium started to nurse hope.

Atlanta, moving on the offense, flopped their drive after Matt Ryan was knocked down by Patriots' linebacker Hightower, with defensive tackle Alan Branch recovering the ball on the Falcons' 25-yard line. Brady only needed five plays to throw another touchdown pass, this one just a six-yard throw to wide receiver Danny Amendola. Then, White took a direct snap-in for a two-point conversion to make the score 28–20 in with 5:56 left on the clock.

Brady's next pass to Amendola gained 20 yards to The Falcons' 21-yard line as the clock ran down below the two-minute warning. Two more passes from Brady to White gained 20 yards and gave the Patriots a first down at the 1-yard line. With 58 seconds left, White scored on a 1-yard touchdown run, and Brady completed a two-point conversion pass to Amendola, tying the score at 28 points apiece to level the 25-point deficit. The game everyone thought was finished had sprung to life and was going to overtime.

New England won the overtime coin toss, flew 75 yards down the field in eight plays, and White, who after being hit by a Falcons defender at the 1-yard line, managed to stretch forward and get the ball across the goal line before his knee hit the ground, scoring the winning touchdown.

The Patriots had won, and Brady had done it again.

Chapter One: The Early Days

Tom's Early Childhood and Family

Every moment of Brady's life has always been for the game.

One of the most incredible sports stars to ever grace sports in its entirety, Brady was born to play football, even though it took a while for the world to recognize it. In the morning of August 3, 1977, Brady was brought into the world by Galynn and Tom Brady Sr. He was their fourth child and only son. The joy was apparent in the family with the young man's arrival, but none of them knew he would become a future NFL star.

Growing up with the guidance of three older sisters, Brady seemed to be under threat of becoming a Cinderella kind of guy. However, a closer look showed that wasn't going to be the case, as his sisters themselves were deeply engrossed with the thrill of sports. The Brady girls, Julie, Maureen, and Nancy were all sports enthusiasts, and so were their parents, which meant a young Brady only had one way to go.

Brady grew and learned the rituals of the family. Every week during the football season, they would all gather to watch the football games and give support to any team whose wins would help the San Francisco 49ers when they were not playing. Tom naturally began developing an interest in sports and enjoyed it.

At first, he would watch everything from basketball to baseball, but as he grew older, he started paying more attention to just football and baseball.

Brady was known to follow his athletic sisters everywhere, including watching their school games at a young age. His three sisters played all major sports, including football, baseball, softball, and basketball. Brady's self-imposed job was to cheer them on, which he did pretty loudly, and to the glee of older supporting locals who gave him the nickname "little Brady." Brady's sisters were highly competitive, and it is believed that this is where he first began developing the spirit of competitiveness and resilience that later characterized his playing style.

Raised as a Catholic, Brady had his personality and life cultured by his neighborhood in San Mateo, where everyone knew each other. He grew into a country boy who loved to hang out with his dad when not watching games with his sisters.

The Bradys were traditional. It was taboo to use foul words and curses, and saying grace before meals was a must.

California was a football mecca, and it didn't take long for Brady to play his first game with kids around the block. Brady also attended games with his dad and developed a soft spot for his dad's team, the 49ers, which subsequently became his childhood love.

Parents and Siblings

Each member of this special family played a role in igniting Brady's passion for football. The Bradys were athletic, with sports being a way of life. Tom has consistently emphasized his family's significant influence on his success.

Thomas Brady Sr.

Thomas Brady Sr. is descended from Irish refugees who migrated to San Francisco from Boston during the great potato famine just before the Civil War. Thomas's family played a part in World War II with his Uncle, Michael Buckley Jr, being the first American prisoner of war.

Thomas graduated from the University of San Francisco with a degree in sociology. He worked for eight years before founding and heading an insurance firm, Thomas Brady and Associates. He is still the company chairman to date. He opened an office in Boston and New York City and stated that his goal was to reach more families and help them plan their insurance needs by putting forth the same level of commitment he had done with his family.

Thomas, now 72, Revealed to *Sports Illustrated* that he had always emphasized the importance of family sticking and doing everything together, and instilled the same belief in Tom from an early age. He stated that he encouraged Brady to follow the ways of the average San Mateo family, as maintaining the family structure would be all he ever needed in life. He was also a season Football ticket holder and regularly took his son to games.

He revealed how delighted he was when his son came out of high school as a success and was recruited by the University of Michigan. However, he also found the recruitment tough due to the distance his son would have to travel away from him. He tried to convince Brady to stay and suggested that he attend Cal-Berkeley, which was about thirty-five miles away, but Brady was set to take the high road.

Thomas is very outspoken, especially when it comes to his son and the NFL in general, though he stated that he never meddled with Tom's career in any phase by trying to advocate for him or advise his coaches.

Galynn Brady

Not much is known about Brady's mom as she has not been in the media as much as her husband. However, she is an avid supporter of her son and is the backbone of the family.

Galynn Brady was born and raised on a dairy farm in Browerville, Minnesota, where her family had settled after leaving Germany. She is of German, Polish, Norwegian, and

Swedish ancestry and was very independent at a young age. She met Tom Brady Sr. when working for Northwest Airlines, and their relationship soon blossomed into marriage. She moved with Tom to San Mateo, California, where they still live today.

Galynn gave birth to her first daughter, Maureen, and soon followed with two other girls, Nancy, and Julie. Each daughter was introduced to sports at a young age and encouraged to pursue a career. Brady was born three years after Julie. Though all four children were born in San Mateo, Galynn took them to visit her relatives in Browerville every summer.

Galynn remains a full-time housewife and regularly plays golf. She staunchly supports whatever profession her kids wanted to choose.

She always urged a young Brady to follow his sisters to watch their games which he was happy to oblige, and she was also a front seat supporter when he made it to the biggest stages of his career. Galynn leads a tranquil life and never went into the news for any personal reasons throughout her over 50 years of marriage with Tom Sr. The only time she was at the center of attention was when her family revealed she had an undisclosed illness in 2016.

The illness affected Brady, who broke down in tears in an after-game interview where he asked for prayers for his mom. The sickness left Galynn unable to watch any of the AFC division games in 2016. Days into the 2017 Superbowl playoff, Galynn was in the front row when the New England Patriots won against the Atlanta Falcons. She later revealed that she had been diagnosed with stage 2 cancer at the start of 2016.

She spoke more on the disease in an October interview, stating, "I remember sitting in the doctor's office and them telling me 'You have breast cancer and it's only stage 2.' The cancer I had was very fast-growing and aggressive. It was going to require a lot of chemotherapy and radiation. And so, the journey began."

Galynn, currently 77, has been doing well and has returned to playing golf.

Maureen Brady

Being the eldest Brady, Maureen had always had the toughest responsibility to deliver on her potential, especially with two ambitious athletic sisters tailing her. From a young age, Maureen had always been athletic like her parents and set the same framework for her younger siblings, who followed the same steps. She played all kinds of sports, including baseball, football, and basketball, and was a popular figure both in school and at home.

Maureen has acknowledged the fact that there was a healthy competition among themselves, with each sibling trying to outdo the other. She revealed that her parents provided that support system, pushing them to chase their ambitions. They passed the same work ethic on to her brother. He learned quickly and, in high school, was keen on outdoing his sisters in sports. She talked about a time when Tom was in the ninth grade, and she and her sisters were always in the local newspapers for their sporting successes. At the time, Tom Brady was recognized by everyone in the neighborhood as Maureen's baby brother or *little Brady*. She stated that he wrote her a message telling her that one day, the three of them would be referred to as Tom Brady's sisters, and he would be a household name.

Maureen praises her family's support system and how it helped build them to strive to always stay at the top. She believes that it was the system that helped motivate Brady to go beyond San Mateo, California, to become the star he now is. "He was always looking to be better, to live up to our expectations, and not disappoint Dad and Mum."

Maureen was an all-American pitcher at Fresno State in the 1990s and could have pushed further, but she had a different career in mind and turned her attention to nursing. She currently works at a local hospital in Bakersfield and has a daughter, Maya, who plays softball at UCLA.

Tom, in an interview, praised her for always having his back and laying down the groundwork for a competitive rivalry.

Nancy Brady

Nancy is the second daughter and, just like her elder sister, competed in sports in high school. She enjoyed considerable success as a softball and basketball player and also often featured in local newspapers. She was also a model figure for Tom and encouraged him to pursue a career in football after his high school success.

Nancy is the most private of the four siblings and has avoided the media since getting married in 2015.

Julie Brady

Julie is the most vibrant of the three sisters, and right from their young age was Tom's closest sibling and ally. She and Tom share the same birth date, and the family jokingly refers to them as twins.

Brady was closer to Julie as a child than his other sisters and listened to her more than anyone except his father. Tom has revealed that she had a significant influence on him growing up. She was an athlete and could play almost every sport like her sisters. She, however, diverted from chasing a sports career after high school.

Julie is currently married to Kelvin Youlis, a former professional baseball player. Her marriage to Youlis is her second. She revealed that Tom was excited when he found out she would marry an athlete and endorsed the union.

Julie, in an interview, spoke about her closeness to her brother, stating that he had been very protective of her and supported her decision to marry Youlis even though he was worried about her ever getting hurt again. She said Tom was a tough kid growing up and was never overwhelmed by responsibilities to meet expectations as a young man.

Julie lives with her husband and kids and has been married since 2012.

Brady has acknowledged that his family was not the average American home and saw strength in togetherness. He once explained about his family, "It was just great to grow up in a house like that and feel so supported by your mom and dad. I've always had that great support at home. I certainly wouldn't be standing here if I didn't have the love and support of my parents and my sisters and my family."

Chapter Two: The First Signs

Surrounded by a family that loved football, Brady was barely in elementary school when he began spotting football role models and idols. His father, who attended the 49er's home games, always took him along, and it was at one of those games that Brady met his idol Joe Montana, the star quarterback for the San Francisco 49ers. He and his father consistently attended the 49ers games at candlestick park, and they were at the 1984 game against the Dallas Cowboys when Joe Montana threw the pass to wide receiver Dwight Clark to earn one of the most memorable victories in NFC history.

Only four years old at the time of the catch, Tom's interest increasingly went to football, and he began practicing plays similar to that of Montana. Also a fan of Steve Young, he became much more determined to excel at playing football. Despite not having many people to play with at home at the time, he began practicing however he could, with whoever would join him. He would also attend football camps hosted by the College of San Mateo, and learned how to throw the football from the camp counselor, getting later tips from NFL/AFL quarterback Tony Graziani. Tony was so surprised by how far Brady could throw that he became serious about becoming Tom's first trainer.

Brady became so engrossed with the game that he was going to football games or watching them on television whenever he was not playing football himself. At this time, he was attending St. Gregory Elementary School, and was able to manage football and studies with his parent's help. He also began to participate in school sports and played flag football and touch football. He played as a quarterback in all of the games and easily outclassed other kids so much that he was noticed by his teachers, who suggested to his parents that they should encourage him in pursuing a career as a player if he continued with the same form.

With support from his parents, trainer, and school, Brady gained more confidence and began aiming to be as good as his sisters and surpass them.

High School

After graduating from St. Gregory Elementary, Tom's parents began searching for the best high school that would help Tom maximize his potential, and eventually settled for San Mateo Serra High School. This all-boys Catholic school was known to have quite a good football program. At this point, Brady was quite good with baseball and touch football, an offshoot of football. He started playing football, basketball, and baseball in his first year in Serra, but stood out in football and baseball and focused on the two. He was recruited into both school teams and as quarterback for football and catcher for baseball. His parents advised him to pick one and give total concentration to prevent burnout, but he chose both teams and was amazingly able to manage them well.

Brady played his first organized football in the first year, but couldn't sustain a starting role and had to sit out two years as a backup quarterback. He was extremely frustrated with his lack of game time but used the opportunity to learn. He finally became the starting quarterback in his junior year. While not good enough to start, the primary quarterback picked up an injury leaving his coach with no choice. At the time, the team struggled and had not scored any touchdowns all year.

Tom, given his chance, took a different approach to the game, and played by relying on his strong throws. He had never been the fastest in his position and knew he would not have much success trying to outrun an opposing team's safety. He, however, could read games, and was a very accurate passer. His new approach brought a refreshing quality to the school's team, the Prades, and they were able to salvage a couple of wins before the end of the season. The football team's turn of fortune led to him cementing his position as the team's starting quarterback, and he kept the role until graduation. His setting of new records earned him a high school rival in Pat Burrell, another promising quarterback from Bellarmine College Preparatory, who also excelled in football and baseball.

Brady enjoyed relative success with the Prades, but they never qualified for the playoffs, and ended up receiving several heavy losses. The first came in Brady's Junior season when Archbishop Mitty blasted Serra 44-0. His team also suffered another heavy defeat, and one of the biggest in high school football history, when they suffered a 63-6 loss to an Eric Brynes led St. Francis team.

Despite these losses in high school, Tom was well known throughout San Francisco as a unique talent. He also gave them better finishes in his two seasons as starting quarterback compared to the first two of his years starting on the bench. He led them to a 6-4 overall finish and 2-3 in the West Catholic Athletic League in his junior year and a 5-5 and 2-3 record in his senior year. While these win-loss results were not enough to take the Prades to the playoffs in Brady's days, it would have been different in modern times with the current 15 divisions in high school football. Nevertheless, Brady set several impressive records, and began showing the first signs of a potential star. He passed for 2,121 yards in 10 games in 1994 and completed a high school career total of 236 of 447 passes for 3,702 yards and 31 touchdowns.

His fame brought him a lot of interest from different observers, but no concrete offer was made as he was yet to graduate. His ability to throw the ball with extreme accuracy and strength placed him ahead of most players his age, and even some quarterbacks in college football. His passing-heavy approach made him stand out from most quarterbacks, and interest in him became more serious and concrete.

Interest in Brady was not only coming from football, as he was just as good in baseball. People who knew him back in school admitted Brady was better at baseball than in football, and was more acknowledged as a baseball player in Serra. He was a left-handed batting catcher with power. He was so good that he attracted different MLB scouts, willing to recruit him into pro baseball. In his senior year, he was drafted in the 18th round of the 1995 MLB Draft by the Montreal Expos. The Montreal Expos projected that he had what it took to become a potential All-Star and offered him a starting salary in the same range as a late second round or early third-round pick.

The draft naturally placed Tom in a peculiar position. He loved football, but had not got any tangible recognition. He also loved baseball, and though not as much as football, he was presented with a chance to be a professional with excellent pay. He, however, didn't take long to make his decision. He wanted to play football, it was all he cared about, and he would chase it and get a college to recruit him.

With the end of his senior year and time at high school fast approaching, he began creating highlight tapes of his best quarterback performances and sent a copy to all the colleges he considered attending. Within a week of sending the videos, he received offers from different football programs around the nation. Many highly rated colleges expressed interest, including the University of California Los Angeles, University of Southern California, University of Michigan, and the University of Illinois. Brady, who had not expected such results, sought advice from his dad. His dad, who wanted his son to stay close to home so he could regularly watch him play, quickly opted for Cal-Berkeley, after they had narrowed the list of possible colleges to five. Brady, however, had Michigan in mind, and ultimately picked it over Cal-Berkeley. This broke his dad's heart, as he felt he was about to lose his best friend.

Before his recruitment by different colleges, Brady was already on Blue-Chip Illustrated and a prep football report All-American Selection. Also, at this time, recruiting was different from the 2000s as athletes' rankings were not as prominent as they are now. Brady would have been considered a four-star recruit with today's system, which meant he was a highly rated prospect. Brady graduated from high school in 1995, with the ceremony held at St. Mary's Cathedral.

In recent times, people who knew Brady in high school have stated that he was a cool person who, despite being very popular with both the football and baseball team, was easily accessible, and was very humble for a star quarterback.

Some football observers who watched him play back then have said that Brady's style wasn't so different from how he has continued to play. Mike Janda, Bellarmine's football coach, explained that Brady has not changed. He revealed that he had pulled out a film of one of his team's games against Brady's 1994 Serra High School team, which the Prades won 27-22, and saw the same stance and motion Brady now possesses. "It's really amazing. You see the quick release, the poise, the accuracy, the strength of the arm. So effortless and smooth the way he threw the ball in high school. In our game—and this is sad—we decided as a coaching staff, and not doing it very smartly, we were going to play a lot of man coverage. That was not a good thing. Our guys played their hearts out. You can watch it on film. They were right with the guys."

Brady had won the All-State and All-Far West honors as well as the Prades team's Most Valuable Player award during the end of his High School career. He was also placed in the Junipero Serra High School Hall of Fame in 2003, his name appearing alongside other legends such as Barry Bonds, Lynn Swann, Gregg Jefferies, and Jim Fregosi, among many others.

Brady was officially recruited by Michigan Assistant Bill Harris and formally signed to play for the University of Michigan in Ann Arbor in 1995.

Chapter Three: College Years

College Career

There are several defining moments and phases in Brady's life, but none were as influential as his college years. After celebrating his college recruitment in a big family way, Brady was headed to Ann Arbor with promises from his parents to watch every game he played. It was approximately 2,407 miles from California to Michigan. Still, he knew his parents were always going to come.

He met Head Coach Lloyd Carr for their first training and, alongside other freshmen, received the ritual pep talk. He noticed that some other quarterbacks had been recruited, and they all seemed to have outstanding high school records. He knew that he would have to compete for his place, and he was ready to do so. After selection and depth rearrangement, he started his career as the team's 7th quarterback. At the time, junior Brian Griese, a future NFL quarterback star, was the Wolverines' starting quarterback. After Michigan's main starter, he had gotten his chance after Scott Driesbach got injured five games into the season.

Griese played most of the games in 1995 in Brady's first year, and when he was not playing, other quarterbacks up the depth list were handed playing time. Brady did not get any time on the field throughout that season and was continuously shadowing other seasoned quarterbacks. During the holidays, he was frustrated and concerned about his lack of game time. He was also worried about Griese and Driesbach, who were heading to their junior and 3rd year, respectively. At the time, he was also working odd jobs to help cover expenses. Some of the jobs were so rigorous it left him tired all through the day, which affected his dedication to training. In one of the jobs, which he has described as his worst, he was made to clean roofs, windows, and floors which left him numb for days.

The 1996 season was no better for Brady as it kicked off with Driesbach and Griese fighting for the position of starting quarterback. Driesbach, who was back from injury, was reinstalled as the team's starting quarterback, while Griese returned to the bench as backup quarterback. Driesbach, however, struggled during the season, and Griese again took up the position of starting quarterback and held the position till the end of the season. This left Brady, who had moved up the chart to third quarterback, competing for the backup quarterback role with Driesbach. Carr, however, mostly went with Driesbach when he had to take off Griese. This left Brady anxious and frustrated. He felt the head coach was deliberately ignoring him despite his training stats being better than Driesbach. Carr mostly ignored his complaints and told him to develop his style of play. At the end of the season, he was featured in only one game after coming from the bench in the fourth quarter. He threw five passes with three completions. After the game, Brady felt he was only playing as an act of pity, and so as not to go the whole season without game time. The season ended on another frustrating note for him.

In the 1997 season, Griese, who had racked up a string of wins for the team the previous season, regained his position as the starting quarterback. Carr noticed Brady had developed his game style and was much more accurate with passes, but Griese was also in excellent form and stuck with him for the season. Griese led the team to an undefeated season and crowned it up with a victory at the Rose Bowl. The win meant Michigan's first-ever championship victory in 49 years, and Carr justified his decision to make Griese the number one man. Brady again spent most of the season on the bench and only had 15 passes with 12 completions to give him an 80 percent accuracy.

Extremely perplexed that his parents and his sisters were always coming from San Mateo to watch him play, despite not getting game time, Brady began slumping and even had to hire a sports psychologist to help him cope. After spending some time with the psychologist, Brady spoke with his dad about transferring to his state university at Cal-Berkeley. His dad told him that he was with him irrespective of the decision he took. After the meeting, Brady then confronted Carr and told him he would be transferred due to his lack of game time, decreasing his chances of becoming an NFL star. Carr, without any reaction, asked what his dad thought about the decision. Brady told him that his dad would support whatever decision he made. Carr, who was seemingly tired of Brady brooding, told him to stop complaining and concentrate on the cause of his woes by fighting for his place. In a 2017 interview, Brady recalls the conversation where the head coach had said, "You know, Tommy, you've gotta worry about yourself. You've gotta go out and worry about the way you play. Not the way the guys ahead of you are playing, not the way your running back is playing, and not the way your receiver ran the route." Brady, still keen on transferring, felt he had to show Carr that he was great and would earn the starting position with him as the coach. Brady told him he was going to prove to him that he was a great quarterback.

Brady began working closely with Assistant Athletic Director, Greg Harden, who believed Brady had tremendous potential to become a top star. He would meet Brady every week to build his confidence and maximize his performance whenever he got to play. Brady explained to *60 Minutes* in 2014, "He will always be somebody I rely on for sound advice and mentorship. He has helped me with my struggles in both athletics and life. Greg pushed me in a direction that I wasn't sure I could go."

With the 1997 season ending, Brady dedicated most of his time to training. He practiced his throws, developed his speed, and studied the quarterbacks. Griese had graduated, and he only had Driesbach to compete with. Before the season began, he outplayed Driesbach and was assigned as starting quarterback for the first time after two seasons. It seemed everything fell into place, and Brady continued to maintain high-level fitness practicing on his own. However, his relief was short-lived when he was told before the new season that he would have to share starting roles with Henson Drew. The announcement dealt a considerable blow to Brady's pride, not because of the change in plans, but because Henson Drew was a freshman.

Drew, who graduated from Brighton High, was a red-hot talent in both football and baseball. He had set national records with 70 home runs, 10 grand slams, 290 RBIs, and a peak speed of 93-mph. He also threw fifty-three touchdown passes in his last three high school seasons. Drew had been highly recruited by many major baseball teams, with the Yankees offering as much as $2 million to get him as a third baseman. Carr, however, had been able to convince Dan, Drew's Dad, and a fellow college football coach, to get his son to sign with the team. Dan agreed on the condition that his son would be the starting quarterback and allowed to feature for the Yankees part-time. The deal meant Brady, a senior by two years, would become the backup for a freshman. However, Brady was so impressive in training that Carr changed his plan and decided to split the role 50-50 between him and Drew. Brady, aware of the younger man on his tail, trained harder and got better with each game. Drew also impressed, putting Carr in a dilemma: how could he restructure and avoid side-lining Brady. Finally, he decided that Brady would start games and Drew would come in later.

Brady, who had resolved to keep the top spot, took his chances, and in that season set Michigan records for most pass attempts and completions in a season. He made a total of 323 passes and completed 214 while also leading the Wolverines in a 31-16 loss against Ohio, one of the few losses in that season, setting a school record for pass completion in a single game. That same season he led Michigan to the Big Ten Conference title and was among its honorable mentions. He also led his team to a 45–31 victory over Arkansas in the Citrus Bowl. During the victories, Brady's relationship with Carr significantly improved, and though he was sharing game time with Drew in every match, he was having more time than the freshman. Drew also held his weight, which still left Carr wondering if Brady's improvement was sustainable and if he could be a better choice than Drew.

Dan began to express disappointment and continuously reminded Carr of his promise to play his son, or they would consider other options. Carr, who was unwilling to let go of Drew, praised the freshman in the subsequent game interview and called him the best talent he had in his team. However, the Michigan fans who had at first preferred Drew to Brady were increasingly warming up to the idea that Brady could just be as good as the great quarterbacks who played before him.

Brady developed a routine during the 1998 season. At night, he would go to Schembechler Hall, the team's football facility, and watch past Wolverine matches. He checked if the opposing coaches in the film were still leading the teams and if most players then still played for the team. He set up schemes to understand the common tendencies of opposing players. He studied the patterns of opposing coaches and how they chose to approach different kinds of opponents. He continued this practice into his senior season, where his development became increasingly noticeable.

The head coach, seeing Brady's improved intelligence, felt more confident with him and, at the start of the 1999 season, retained him as the starting quarterback to the ire of Dan, who felt their deal was being breached. Carr also revealed to Dan that he could no longer come to Drew's training as he became a distraction to him and the entire team. He stayed away, but only sort of. While he never appeared on the sidelines, he was often spotted watching the training from under the bridge or from the shade.

Before the opener of the season, Carr, wanting to start Brady and keep Drew, decided on a compromise. Brady would start and play the first quarter, while Henderson would play the second quarter. At halftime, the coaches would pick which person finishes the game. This decision irritated Brady, who believed it was a move to cut his playing time, and could have drastic consequences for his chance of making it to the NFL. He felt unfairly treated by Carr but didn't complain. He was already in his senior year and had to make do.

The first five games started with Brady as quarterback in the second half and team leader. The Wolverines won all five, including memorable wins over Notre Dame and against powerhouse Wisconsin while on the road.

In the next game against Michigan State, Brady was dropped for Drew in the second half, and the offense fell apart. Carr quickly reinstated Brady when the team fell behind by a 17 point deficit and staged a potential comeback which only fell short by three points with the game ending 34-31. They again lost their next game against Illinois after blowing a 20-point lead earned by Brady during Drew's quarter. The following week, Brady covered 300 yards with his passes, and Carr exclusively assigned him as the team's starting quarterback.

Brady's ability to read his teammates and his opponents' plays excelled. He knew which receiver would be open and knew how opponents would line up. He also developed what became his hallmark, an extreme calmness, and accuracy when he was about to get hit. After a bad game, he would go through every incompletion and tell his teammates what cost them the game; wrong route, lousy throw, wrong read, missed block, and when the film of the said game was reviewed, his analysis would be pinpointed.

Brady, also now enjoying more game time, led the Wolverines to a string of wins, including multiple comebacks in the fourth quarter, including a remarkable win against Penn State in a game characterized by blood and sweat. In the first half of the game, Brady threw three interceptions and was sacked multiple times. At the end of the half, he was bleeding from a cut on his face. His team receiver David Terrell exclaimed when he saw the cut, and Brady calmly told him not to worry about him and focus on doing his job in the second half. In the fourth quarter of the second half, the Wolverines were trailing Penn State 21-17 before Brady engineered a spirited comeback that saw them win the game 31-34. Speaking to reporters after the game, Brady stated that he knew they were not going to lose.

Brady continued his dominance up to the last game of the regular season against Ohio State, which also ended dramatically. The game that would determine who made the trip to the orange bowl was tied at 17-17 with five minutes left and set for overtime. Brady, however, threw a 25-yard pass to score a winning touchdown. The win earned the team a 9-2 win-loss record, which meant they were heading to the Orange Bowl with Brady leading them. The Wolverines were to face southeastern conference champions, Alabama.

The Orange Bowl saw Brady put on one of his best performances in college football. He threw for 369 yards and four touchdowns and led the Wolverines out of huge deficits in each half. With his team down 14-0, Brady forced a 14-14 tie before the end of the first half, and again repeated the same magic to cause a 28-28 overtime after going down 28-14. He completed an amazing night by throwing the game-winning score to win his second national championship.

The victory made Brady a fan favorite and was highly rated by reporters and the media. The next morning after the game, Wolverine team members celebrated in their hotel. Brady, however, was relatively calm, and when Carr went out to answer reporters, he went into the dining room where his teammates were eating, waved goodbye, and left without saying a word. He was no longer a Wolverine and was heading home. He graduated at the age of 22.

In his two starting seasons, Brady led his team to 20 wins and 5 losses. Most of the wins were earned from a comeback position earning him the nickname "comeback kid." Also, despite not playing as much as most Michigan starting quarterbacks before him, he was still able to finish his career ranking third in the college's history with 710 attempts and 442 completions, fourth with 5351 yards and 62.3% completion, and fifth with 35 touchdown passes. He also won the 1998 Citrus Bowl and the 1999 Orange Bowl.

Many colleges and pro football analysts believed that he would have ranked first in most of the positions if given more game time. Tom Sr. spoke with *Sports Illustrated* about how

Brady's college years were. He revealed that it was a challenging time for Brady due to the frustrations of not getting played. He explained Brady felt horrible every time they came to watch him, only to see him benched for the better part of four years. His father, who was irked during the revelation, stated, "It's a pretty sore spot, to be honest with you. He wasn't treated very kindly by the head coach." Carr also admitted that he never made it easy for Brady, for which he felt bad. "He had some tough challenges because of the position that I put him in." A more matured Brady has often preferred not to talk about his college years in interviews as it upsets him most times.

Brady's college days' lows and highs were what ultimately prepared him for the more formidable challenges he would face on his way. The side-lining by the head coach resulted in him training and honing his skills, creating his calmness and concentration when hitting pinpoint passes, even when charged at, and his high level of football IQ.

Making The NFL Draft

With his college career done and a BS in general studies completed, Brady was caught in a mix of certainty and uncertainty on what would happen next. He knew he wanted to play football. He, however, had a slight concern: had he done enough in college football to be considered worthy of being picked in next year's draft? He knew he was good, but the pro teams may not see that after being benched for two full seasons, and when given a chance to play, he had to share it with a first-year student. He had won twenty of the twenty-five games he started, and he knew he could throw very well, but would that be enough for him to be considered in pro football? His family, however, believed he had a great chance, and should be among the top selections as he had done very well in his final two seasons, which was the most important thing. While waiting for the draft, Brady spent most of his time sightseeing California and developing his skills, something that had become a part of his daily routine.

On the day of the first draft, everyone in the house was expectant, and even Brady was feeling good. He believed he would be picked. He had discussed this with Greg Harden, who had become his friend and his go-to counselor. Greg had assured him that he had done enough to be selected, so he didn't worry as much as he did at first. He was pacing calmly while the first round commenced. The round lasted for hours, and when it was over, he had not been selected by any team. He wasn't exactly disappointed as he knew he didn't have the best scouting combine before the draft. However, he could sense the tension in his family.

The second and third round came three days later, and he still wasn't picked. He began to feel the reality of the situation.

Some of his college teammates, who he felt had worse chances than him, had already been selected, and he still had not been considered. His dad reassured him not to worry and looked forward to the remaining rounds. He didn't want to believe his advice, but he would hold on to it since it was coming from his dad. The fourth and the fifth round came, and his name was not still not called. For him, reality set in. He was not playing football. Quarterbacks mostly get picked in the first three rounds, and it was already past the fifth round.

On the day of the sixth round, Brady had lost all hope of being picked and went out for a stroll while his family cramped up at home, praying he got called. Brady stayed out until nightfall. He didn't know how long he had been out or how many times he had cried, but when Julie called to tell him he had been picked, he felt elated. He was going to play football.

Brady was drafted by the New England Patriots franchise and was the 199th player picked and the seventh quarterback overall. He received a call from the franchise the following day that he had been drafted, and he thanked the caller for the privilege. After the call, he went to work immediately. The Patriots were in the AFC Division and had not won a title for a long time. He, however, cherished his chance to continue playing football.

Chapter Four: The NFL

New England Patriots (Stirring Up a Tired Team)

While Brady already knew the Patriots weren't one of the top teams, he didn't know that the team was such a mess. The Patriots in 2000 had sacked the previous coach and installed a new coach with a new crop of management, hoping to turn their fortunes around. He discovered that his drafting was a stroke of luck, and the management didn't actually want a quarterback. They only picked him because of his unique approach to games, as they thought his style may be something they could use. He wasn't number one, but it barely mattered to him.

Walking down the stairs of Foxboro Stadium, the first person Brady met was Robert Kraft, the franchise owner. He didn't know how to react, as he stood face to face with the man who had made all this possible. He wasn't sure how to address him, and in the end, went with Mr. Kraft. He tried to explain who he was, but before he could, Robert interrupted and told him he knew who he was. Tom Brady and their sixth pick. Brady smiled, knowing the implication. He wasn't picked because they expected anything super from him. He was going to show them their indifferent decision was the best they made. He looked Robert Kraft in the eye and told him that he would prove he was the franchise's best decision.

Brady got introduced to his teammates the same day and met with the Head Coach Bill Belichick, who welcomed him. He went through the team talk with the other new recruits and then got work. He already knew Drew Bledsoe was the starting quarterback and John Friesz was the backup. Then there was Michael Bishop as the third option. Brady was fourth, but that didn't matter much to him. All he needed to do was outperform every single one of them and become number one. That was how he got it done at college, and he was going to do it there.

He immediately made friends with Bledsoe and consistently pelted him with questions. The big man was more than willing to teach Brady, and he took notes. During games, Brady was never bothered with his lack of playing time, and was more concerned about how each teammate played, how the receiver and tight end moved and arranged themselves, and how the coach set up his playing style. He started hitting the gym when he found out his 204-pound frame was a source of concern for his coaches. He added an additional 16 pounds to help him achieve sufficient NFL size. He watched videos and tried to see what they did wrong and where the fault consistently came from. He built a reputation for throwing accurate passes in training. However, Belichick kept quiet.

On November 23, Brady got his first call up for the season, coming in for Bledsoe in the fourth quarter against the Detroit

Lions. A little surprised that he had been picked over Friesz and Bishop, Brady tried to impress with the few minutes he had and was able to complete one pass out of 3 attempts with tight end Rod Rutledge receiving. The Patriots finished at the bottom of their division, setting an all-time low record of 5-11.

During the off-season, Brady focused on everything he had learned. His improvements were so great that at the 2001 training camp, he was pointed out as one of the team's healthiest and most improved players. Belichick and the other coaches were so impressed that they named him backup quarterback to Drew Bledsoe. At the time, the Patriots' fans had been publicly showing their dissatisfaction with Bledsoe and asked that Bishop start.

Becoming The New England Patriots Starting Quarterback

The new season began with Bledsoe as the starting quarterback and the Patriots playing on the road against the Cincinnati Bengals. Bledsoe completed the game, which ended with the Patriots losing by 23-17. This led to more cries from fans who had been asking for Bledsoe to be benched. Despite the pressure, Belichick stuck with Bledsoe for the next game, which was also the first home game for The Patriots on September 23.

The Patriots were squaring off against the New York Jets, and Bledsoe played the game till the fourth quarter which began with the Patriots down 10-3. With only a few minutes remaining, Bledsoe received the ball and attempted to run with it but got tackled by Jets linebacker Mo Lewis, who collided with the quarterback and left the Patriots' star flattened. Officials attended to Bledsoe, who had to be taken off the field on a stretcher. The coach sent in Brady. The Jets held on to their lead, with the Patriots recording a 0-2 start to the season.

That same day, Bledsoe was confirmed to have suffered from internal bleeding, which would rule him out for most of the season. This made Brady the starting quarterback, despite analysts and fans predicting Bishop or John would be the replacement. Brady played the next game as starting quarterback for the first time against the Indianapolis Colts and rallied the team to a 44-13 win, which left Peyton Manning, the Colts quarterback, stunned. Then, the Patriots won their fourth game with an even better display as Brady found his stride. With two impressive wins, fans began expressing support for the coach's decision to start a sixth-round quarterback.

The support helped Brady adapt quickly as the team's starting quarterback and he impressed everyone in the fifth game against the San Diego Chargers. The Patriots were trailing 26-16 at the fourth quarter before Brady made two scoring drives to force overtime. He set up another scoring drive to set up a winning field goal in overtime, provoking memories of his comeback performances in college. He finished the game with 54 passes and completed 33 for 364 yards and scored two touchdowns. His performance in the game earned him the AFC Offensive Player of the Week for just his third game as starting quarterback. The Patriots, formerly among the bottom teams with two starting defeats, were catapulted to mid-table. The following week, in a rematch at Indianapolis against the Colts, Brady again gave a world-class performance with a passer rating of 148.3 to condemn the Colts to a 38–17 loss. The Patriots continued their winning streak, finishing the season with eleven wins and 5 losses.

The turnaround made the Patriots the champions of the AFC East, and was Brady the name on every American's lips, football lovers or not. The championship win meant The Patriots were set for the 2001-2002 NFL playoffs with a first-round bye, a feat that was unlikely at the start of the season. Brady finished the season with 2,843 passing yards and 18 touchdowns, which was enough to earn him an invitation to the 2002 Pro Bowl.

During the playoffs, Brady, in the first game against the Oakland Raiders, threw for 312 yards to force a comeback from a ten-point deficit in the fourth quarter, sending the game to overtime, and won the match with an Adam Vinatieri goal in a game that was filled with stops and controversies. He finished the game with 32 completed passes out of 52 attempts.

During the AFC Championship Game that would qualify them for a shot at the Super Bowl, Brady picked up a knee injury and was replaced by a recovered Bledsoe. The Patriots won 24-17 to qualify for Super Bowl XXXVI against the NFC's New York Giants and would go on to meet the defending champions, the St. Louis Rams.

Qualifying for the Super Bowl led to a celebration in the team and among the Patriots fans who had not had many experiences with the NFL's main event. Before Brady's wonder-changing season, they had only gone to The Bowl twice, and had lost both times. For them, the progress was an unexpected and significant move that promised a lot in the future, but that was it. They didn't expect the team to win, and it wasn't only them. Even analysts predicted that a victory at the Super Bowl was improbable. The Rams were a top dog team with multiple players who already had Superbowl rings. Compared to a resurging team led by an inexperienced quarterback, it was expected to go only one way. Las Vegas oddsmakers positioned The Patriots as 14-point underdogs.

Brady, unlike everyone else, was extremely calm, and expressed indifference in the middle of the noise and speculations. He didn't feel that they were underdogs and saw it as just a typical game.

On the day of the match, Brady was so calm that he fell asleep a few hours before the game. When he woke up, he told himself that it was just another football game. The game kicked off with the Patriots in front, stunning St. Louis while holding back their powerful offense throughout the first half. The second half commenced in the same fashion, with the Patriots scoring more points while keeping the Rams at bay. The Patriots defense maintained a 17-3 lead into the fourth quarter. However, the formation fell apart, and with 1:30 minute remaining, The Rams tied the game. The Rams went on to hold back the Patriots. The Patriots, who had the ball at their 17-yard line, had the opportunity to run out the clock and force overtime. Brady, however, had another plan, and set up a fantastic nine-play drive down the field of the Rams 31-yard line before spiking the ball with seven seconds left. Patriot Kicker Adam Vinatieri then converted a 48-yard field goal at the end of time to ultimately beat St. Louis 20-17 and give the Patriots their first-ever Superbowl win!

After the win, Brady was named Super Bowl MVP, his first title in his very first Super Bowl appearance. He threw for 145 yards, had one touchdown, and no interceptions. The win turned all of Boston into celebration. Brady himself was the NFL dream boy as he had achieved in one season what many seasoned quarterbacks dreamt of their entire careers. At the age of 24, he was the youngest quarterback to win a Super Bowl, breaking the record of Joe Montana, his idol. He also earned an invite from Disney World and was taken for a tour with his mum to celebrate.

Bledsoe was traded to the Buffalo Bills in the off-season, cementing Brady as the Patriots' starting quarterback. Brady achieved his dream during his first season as a starter and went home to celebrate.

The 2003 season started with the Patriots under Brady's leadership and hoping to replicate their success. In their opening game, Brady led them to a 30-14 win against the Pittsburgh Steelers with 294 passing yards and was named the AFC Offensive Player of the Week, his third time being awarded the honor. The Patriots followed up the win with a string of others, and ended the season with a 9-7 win-loss record and tied the New York Jets and Miami Dolphins for the season's best finish. However, the New York Jets won the division title on tiebreakers, leaving Brady and the Patriots with the option of qualifying for the playoffs through the divisional wild card games. They faced the Cleveland Browns for the final wild-card spot, and again lost the tiebreaker, missing the playoffs. The match ended a tough and unlucky season for the team. Brady also registered a career-low-single season passer rating of 85.7 and a career-high of 14 interceptions. Brady's performance at the end of the season became a cause of discussion, with analysts wondering if he would ever repeat his previous success.

However, the following season was redemption for Brady, finding him in red-hot form. He led The Patriots to twelve consecutive victories that started after the team's first four games ended in even wins and losses. Brady broke and set many records for the season. He recorded a 36-yard punt in a 12-0 pummeling of the Miami Dolphins and finished the division games with a total of 3,620 passing yards and 23 touchdowns. They beat the Tennessee Titans and Indianapolis Colts in the divisional round and AFC Championship Game. The wins took them to their second Super Bowl in three years. They faced the Carolina Panthers and won the game 32-29, securing him his second championship in just 3 years!

The following season followed up from exactly where they had stopped, with The Patriots winning their first nine games in a row.

They completed the season with a record 14-2 in what was a repeat of their preceding season. The record made the team the best defending champions in the division's history, and they won the title for the third time with Brady as starting quarterback. Going to the playoffs, Brady led his team to victory against the Indianapolis Colts in the divisional round, 20-3. In the AFC Championship Game, he won against the Pittsburgh Steelers to advance to his second consecutive Super Bowl. Pittsburgh featured one of Brady's best performances for the season, despite being on IV treatment after running a temperature of 103 F the night before the game. He dominated the entire game and recorded a passer rating of 130.5.

In the Super Bowl game, Brady led his team in a nail-biting battle against the Philadelphia Eagles. The match, which had some incredible moments, ended in favor of the Patriots, 24-21, winning them their third championship in four years. They also became the third team in NFL history to do so, with the Dallas Cowboys being the first. Brady, who was again the main man, threw for 236 yards and two touchdowns.

Brady, after the win, told his teammates to prepare for the following season as the aim would be to win the Super Bowl for the third time consecutively. Things, however, didn't go to plan. While the team started brightly, things began to get tricky when three starting running backs were dropped due to injury just before the halfway point of the season. This made the team depend heavily on Brady's passes, which had to adjust to the new running backs. The team struggled toward their third consecutive AFC East title with a 10-6 win-loss record. Brady and the Patriots, however, suffered a disappointing loss at the divisional round against the Denver Broncos. It was later revealed that he had been suffering from a hernia for a better part of the season and up to the playoffs.

The following season, Brady led the Patriots to a 12-4 record, but lost out on the division championship. They did, however, qualify for the playoffs after beating The New York Jets in the wild card round 37-16. The divisional playoff round was held in California, Brady's home state, with the match against the San

Diego Chargers. Brady and his teammates struggled for the better part of the game. Still, he was able to turn the tide by initiating a critical drive that ultimately ended with him throwing a 49-yard pass play to receiver Caldwell, which set up a Stephen Gostkowski field goal to give The Patriots a 24–21 win. However, in the AFC Championship Game, the Patriots succumbed to their first playoff loss against the Indianapolis Colts. The loss meant a trophyless season for Brady.

In the 2007 season, however, the Patriots staged a resurgence with a clean, perfect season that saw them win all of their 16 division games. Brady achieved many milestones and set records for the Patriots and the NFL. He earned the AFC Offensive Player of the Week five times that season, and also got his revenge against the Indianapolis Colts by leading his team to earn a 24-20 comeback win, breaking Peyton Manning's record of eight consecutive three-touchdown games by recording his ninth consecutive game of hat trick touchdowns. He again broke Manning's single-season record of 49 touchdowns by hitting his 50th in the season's final game against the New York Jets. Despite the dominance of the division and the trouncing of the San Diego Chargers in the AFC Championship Game, the Patriots lost their first-ever Super Bowl with Brady as the starting quarterback.

The following season Brady was at the end of a crunching tackle from Kansas City Chiefs' safety Bernard Pollard. It was the season opener and was decidedly Brady's last game of the season when it was revealed that he had torn his anterior cruciate ligament and medial collateral ligament. The injury required surgery, and the procedure was done by renowned surgeon Dr. Neal at the Los Angeles Kerlan-Jobe Orthopaedic Clinic.

Brady returned the following season after marrying his long-time girlfriend, Gisele Bündchen, on February 26, in a private ceremony in Santa Monica. He put up another great performance that season, but it was not until 2015 that he would win his fourth Super Bowl after losing out on the 2011 Super Bowl XLVI. He won his fifth Super Bowl with the Patriots in 2017 in a game that engineered one of the greatest comebacks in sports history against NFC Champions, the Atlanta Falcons. He won his sixth Super Bowl against the Los Angeles Rams two years later to tie Charles Haley as the highest Super Bowl winner, while also becoming the oldest player to win a Super Bowl at 41.

The 2019 season kicked off later in the year, with Brady signing a two-year contract extension lasting until 2021. The contract had a free agent agreement that gave him the freedom to leave the Patriots at the end of the 2019 season. Brady, however, wanted a longer contract, but The Patriot's management, fearing that he was ageing and may not be in good form past 2021, were unwilling to grant his wish. This led to an on and off talk between Brady's management and the Patriots. Despite this, Brady focused on his on-field games and, in the opener against the Pittsburgh Steelers, completed 24 of 36 passes for 341 yards and three touchdowns to beat The Steelers 33-3. He broke several records and, in week 6, overtook Peyton Manning on the all-time passing yards list and was only second to Drew Brees. Despite these records, however, The Patriot's offense was becoming notably stagnant, with Brady being isolated most times. He talked to Belichick about it, but the coach waved it off and stated the offense was just as powerful as it had always been. Brady, frustrated, complained to his friends that Belichick was taking the team offense for granted because they had been good for so long. He predicted that the effects were soon going to show.

Just as Brady predicted, the second half of the season went with the Patriots losing three of their first five games, including back-to-back losses against the Houston Texans, and the Kansas City Chiefs. The last game of the season also ended in a loss against The Miami Dolphins. Nevertheless, the Patriots, who had a perfect 8-0 start, clinched the AFC East title but were denied a first-round bye. Their postseason game on the wild card run saw them face the Tennessee Titans in a tight contest that saw the Patriots trailing 14-13 and pinned to their one-yard line with seconds left in the fourth quarter. In a desperate attempt to gain a lead before time expired, Brady threw a pass that was intercepted and brought back for a touchdown by Titans' cornerback and former Patriot, Logan Ryan. The Titans won 20-13.

Brady, who had been brooding about the team's ailing offense and Belichick's refusal to improve it, began to reconsider his future with the Patriots after spending 20 years with the franchise. He wanted to win, and felt he wouldn't do it with the team's current offense. After consulting with his wife and family during the off-season, Brady, on March 17, 2020, announced that he would not re-sign with the Patriots. His contract expired the following day, officially ending his 20-year dominance in New England.

Brady's announcement to end his stay was met with mixed reactions from fans, with some expressing sadness and others appreciation for the years he had spent with them. Brady was celebrated on both state TV stations and radios while he dominated national headlines. Fans and government institutions set up a total of 11 billboards thanking Brady. The Patriots also honored Brady and acknowledged him as the greatest player to have ever worn the shirt. For Brady, however, he knew what he wanted. He had signed with the Tampa Bay Buccaneers the same day he announced he was leaving the Patriots, and had already started making plans to move to Florida. While he wanted to stay with New England, he felt his era with Belichick had come to an end, and he had to move to face other challenges.

Moving to Florida: Tampa Bay Buccaneers

Brady's signing with the Buccaneers marked his first season for a team with a crop of players he didn't know. He was 42, past his peak, and knew he had to approach the challenge differently. He was more seasoned now and had plenty of experience, but he was also slower than before. Nevertheless, he wanted to win, and he was going to. His contract with the Buccaneers lasted two seasons and was valued at $50 million with $4.5 million in annual incentives, making him the highest-paid player for the team.

While he had worn the number 12 throughout his Patriot days, Brady discovered the number was already assigned to Chris Godwin. Godwin, who had always respected Brady and saw him as an influence, offered the number and switched to 14. Outside Tampa Bay, talks and news about his move were raging, with analysts arguing if he would ever win the Super Bowl or the division title with a team that wasn't really in their best strides. They also worried about his age and the odds of him replicating his success with his former team.

Brady's debut game was against the New Orleans Saints, led by star quarterback Drew Brees. Brady impressed individually by completing 23 of 36 passes for 239 yards, two touchdowns, and had two interceptions. The Saints, however, got the victory, with the game ending 34-23. Brady and the Buccaneers bounced back in their next few games with the fourth one against the Los

Angeles Chargers, where he completed 30 of 46 passes for 369 yards and had five touchdowns. The game also earned Brady the NFC Offensive Player of the Week. Brady's performance earned him praise among football fans, though five weeks later, he suffered the worst defeat of his professional career when his team fell to a 38-3 loss to New Orleans for the second time of the season.

Brady rallied his team to a string of wins but fell short of winning the division title, with the Saints winning it instead. They settled for a wild card spot after trouncing the Detroit Lions with a score of 47-7. The playoff gave them a spot at Super Bowl LV, the 10th Super Bowl appearance for Brady.

Brady dominated the Super Bowl game, with The Buccaneers cruising to a 31-9 win against the Kansas City Chiefs. He also won the MVP of the match after throwing 201 yards, securing three touchdowns, and giving two touchdown passes to tight end Rob "Gronk" Gronkowski, former Patriot teammate and one of Brady's biggest allies. The passes between the duo set a record for most postseason touchdown passes between a passer-receiver for a total of 14, breaking Joe Montana and Jerry Rice's record of 13. The win also meant Brady's seventh Super Bowl victory, setting a record for the most ring wins in the history of the NFL. His MVP Award also helped him extend his NFL record to a total of five. In addition, he extended his record of being the oldest player to start, play, and win the Super Bowl from age 41 to 43.

Brady is still currently signed with the Buccaneers and, while he may not be at his youthful best, is still the starting quarterback.

Notable Career Achievements

Brady's style of play was characterized by his on-field intelligence, excellent pocket awareness, and his ability to stay calm and maintain concentration when throwing passes. As a result, he has broken and set many NFL records, including the most games won by a quarterback with 264, most games played by a quarterback at 346, most games started by a quarterback with 344, most combined passing yards in 91,653, and most combined touchdown passes with 664. He also has the most game-winning drives with 61, most fourth-quarter comebacks with 48, most NFL Championships by a player, with 7, and most championships in Pro Football History by a player, tied with Otto Graham.

Like the NFL, Brady's Super Bowl record is also impressive, with the most notable being the highest Super Bowl wins for a player and a starting quarterback with 7. After winning six for the Patriots and moving to the Buccaneers to win his 7th Super Bowl ring, he became the only player to have more wins than any franchise in the NFL, beating his former team and the Pittsburgh Steelers who had six. He also became the only player to win the Super Bowl in two different conferences, doing so in the AFC and NFC, after moving to the Buccaneers and tying rival Peyton Manning to win the ring for two different teams. In addition, he holds the record for most touchdown passes, 21, most passing yards with 3,039, most passes completed with 277, and most passes attempted with 421, most Super Bowl appearances, having appeared in 10, and with the most game-winning drives with 6.

For the regular season, Brady holds the following notable records: most games won by a quarterback with 230, most games with more than two touchdown passes with 173, most thrown, and most touchdown passes with 77. He is the only quarterback to have three consecutive games with more than 300 passing yards, at least 3 touchdown-passes, and 0 interceptions. He is the oldest player to win an MVP award at the age of 40, and the player with the most career passing yards with one team at 74,571. He holds the record for most career touchdown passes at 581, and is the only quarterback in the NFL to have at least 40 passing touchdowns in a season, having done it twice in the AFC with 50 passes and again in the NFC with the Buccaneers with 40 passes.

Deflategate

Brady was caught in the middle of a ball controversy that came to be called Deflategate in 2015. The controversy began when the NFL published a 243-page report regarding the deflation of footballs in the AFC Championship Game of the 2014 season, which The Patriots won. The report stated that about ¾ of the balls made available for the game were deflated by the Patriots management and did not reach the standard required for an NFL game. The statement also read that this was intentionally done to help Brady with his throws. The report then concluded that Brady, being the team leader, was aware of the deflation, and had condoned the misconduct with his silence. Five days later, the NFL handed Brady a four-game suspension that was to start at the beginning of the 2015 season.

The decision of the NFL to restrict Brady for four games was contained in a report that stated that Brady had been unwilling to help or cooperate with investigators. NFL Executive Vice President of Football Operations, Troy Vincent, then penned an open letter to Brady, which in part read, "Your actions as set forth in the report clearly constitute conduct detrimental to the integrity of and public confidence in the game of professional football." Brady, who claimed not to have been aware of the deflated balls, appealed the suspension on May 14 through the NFL Players Association.

Rodger Goodell, the commissioner of the NFL, again upheld the four-game suspension, explaining that he was disappointed with the report and had chosen to enforce the ban because Brady had destroyed his cell phone, which may have contained evidence. The suspension decision was taken to the federal court for confirmation. In a statement on Facebook, Brady expressed disappointment in Goodell's decisions and criticized it as irrational and factless. Months after the NFL filed papers to confirm the suspension, Judge Richard M. Berman of the United States District Court for the Southern District of New York vacated the suspension and permitted Brady to play the next four games. The ruling, as stated by the judge, was decided because the NFL had failed to give early notice to Brady about the investigation, the charges against him, and the punishment of suspension. The judge also cited that Goodell had manipulated Brady's testimony at the appeal hearing. The revoking of the suspension ruling lasted from July until the end of the 2015 AFC East Division.

The case was again reopened the following year in March after the NFL appealed that the judge should revoke his decision to vacate the suspension as compelling evidence showed that Brady was involved in the scandal. The case was reopened, and on April 25, 2016, the ruling to vacate the four-game suspension was overturned, and the suspension was upheld. Brady accepted the suspension after attempts to trigger another appeal were unsuccessful.

Many reactions trailed the controversy, with many analysts stating that the punishment, while harsh, was fair. Some noted that the Patriots have always bent the rules, and therefore, the suspension would serve as just punishment. Brady's dad, Thomas Sr., was angered by the ruling and publicly criticized Goodell.

Chapter Five: Life Outside of Football

Personal Life

On a personal level, not a lot is known about Brady, despite being a popular figure for over twenty years. Brady, when not playing, enjoys spending time with his family in California. He finally settled in Massachusetts after getting married to supermodel Gisele Bündchen on February 26, 2009. The marriage was a private ceremony that only had the couple's family and few invited friends. Together they have two children: Benjamin and Vivian. Benjamin was born in 2009, while Vivian was born in 2012. Brady had another son, Jack, with his ex-girlfriend Bridget Moynahan before he got married to Bündchen. The family of five all live on Davis Island where *Brady Mansion* is located, though Bridget sometimes takes Jack to her place during the holidays.

Brady revealed in an interview that Jack was like him and wanted to do all the things he loved. He worked hard, played football, and was always concerned about not disappointing him, which he said reminded him of his childhood with his own dad. He would normally hang out with his dad or go to his sister's games without having much time to party or play with friends.

With Benjamin, the case is entirely different. He does not enjoy football, and instead, he loves to hang out with his pals. Brady describes Vivian as the princess of the home who gets whatever she wants.

Politics

For a football star who spent most of his years playing football, Brady is impressively knowledgeable about politics and the political system of the United States. He is a Republican and attended the 2004 state of the union Address after being invited by President George W Bush. That same year, he revealed that being a senator would be his craziest ambition, though he has later come out to state that he would not be going into politics as it and football did not mix well.

Brady is a close friend of Former President Trump and in 2017 stated that he had known the former United States leader for over 16 years. On the eve of the 2016 presidential election, President Trump told voters that Brady had called him to wish him the best. Brady's wife, however, is a Democrat and, when asked in an Instagram live session if she and her husband supported Trump, she answered *NO*. Brady later revealed that after the 2016 election, his wife asked him not to discuss politics publicly. He, however, supported and endorsed Helen Brady for the Massachusetts State Auditor seat.

Non-NFL Endeavors

Brady has been involved in many non-NFL shows and pursuits since his first Super Bowl. He has been featured in *The Simpsons, Entourage, Family Guy,* and has hosted *Saturday Night Live*, all of which he did between 2005 and 2009. In the 2010s, he either made a cameo appearance or played a substantial role in several movies.

Brady has endorsed beauty brands like Stetson Cologne. He has also endorsed other brands, including Movado, Under Armour, Uggs, Glaceau SmartWater, and Aston Martin.

Brady, who has always been a preacher of healthy eating and living, announced the launch of his healthy living and peak performance website TB12sports.com. The site, which is exercise and sport-based, features Brady's training regime and includes a store to purchase TB12 equipment and merchandise. Brady also launched the TB12 Foundation in 2016 to provide free post-injury rehabilitation care and training programs for underprivileged athletes.

On September 19, 2017, under Simon & Schuster, Brady published his first book, *The TB12 Method: How to achieve a lifetime of peak performance*. The book became a number one bestseller on Amazon within 24 hours. It also reached number 1 on the New York Times Best Sellers List.

Influence and Legacy

Brady is the most dominant player in the history of the NFL and has broken almost every quarterback record the organization has. In addition, he is considered the greatest player to have ever worn an NFL jersey, and is consistently called the biggest steal due to his 199th pick in the 2000 NFL draft.

Brady has the highest number of Super Bowl rings with seven and has the highest number of games for a single player. He is also the quarterback with the highest number of wins and has the longest number of consecutive games in NFL history with 112.

Brady Serra High School Stadium was renamed the Brady Family Stadium. In California, Massachusetts, and Florida, many kids have been named Tom Brady, making the name one of the most popular in the United States.

Brady is a future NFL Hall of Fame member and is one of its most influential players, with many quarterbacks and NFL players citing him as an influence and an idol.

Conclusion

As you can see from reading this book, Tom Brady is a once in a generation talent. While he might not be the most naturally gifted or athletic, his work ethic is seemingly unmatched, and that is what has allowed him to enjoy such a long and prosperous career.

As arguably the best player to ever grace the football field, Tom Brady is still going! What the future holds for him is uncertain, though we can be sure that in the next season he will be doing all he can to secure his 8th Super Bowl ring!

I hope you have enjoyed learning about the life and career of Tom Brady, and will enjoy watching him on the field even more now that you know a little bit more about his inspiring journey!

References

Arnold, J. (2012, February 3). *Sister pact: How Tom Brady's special bond with his sisters helped make him a Star.* GoBulldogs. Retrieved February 3, 2022, from https://gobulldogs.com/news/2012/2/3/Sister_Pact_How_Tom_Brady_s_Special_Bond_With_His_Sisters_Helped_Make_Him_A_Star

Contributor, O. (2019, January 30). *Once upon a time, Tom Brady couldn't get his high school team to the playoffs.* Bangor Daily News. Retrieved February 3, 2022, from https://bangordailynews.com/2019/01/30/sports/once-upon-a-time-tom-brady-couldnt-get-his-high-school-team-to-the-playoffs/

Staff, K. N. B. R. (2020, April 8). *Brady talks Montana Comparisons, 'smoking weed' in interview with Howard Stern.* KNBR. Retrieved February 3, 2022, from https://www.knbr.com/2020/04/08/brady-talks-montana-comparisons-smoking-weed-at-serra-high-school-in-interview-with-howard-stern/

Rosenberg, M. (2012, January 9). *Tom Brady as you forgot him - sports illustrated vault.* vault.SI.com. Retrieved February 3, 2022, from https://vault.si.com/vault/2012/01/09/tom-brady-as-you-forgot-him

Fandom. (n.d.). *Tom Brady.* American National Football League Fandom Wiki. Retrieved February 3, 2022, from https://americannationalfootballleague.fandom.com/wiki/Tom_Brady#2001_Season

Ingram Content Group UK Ltd.
Milton Keynes UK
UKHW050732220623
423745UK00022B/404